D0331148

DAO
DE JING

天道

DAO DE JING
THE UNITED VERSION

LAOZI

A NEW TRANSLATION BY
YANG PENG

Wapner & Brent Books
Woodstock, NY

© 2016 Yang Peng

Published by Wapner & Brent Books
PO Box 12, Woodstock, NY 12498

Wapner & Brent Books is a publishing project of the Institute for Publishing Arts, Inc., 120 Station Hill Road, Barrytown, NY 12507, a not-for-profit, tax-exempt organization [501(c)(3)].

Cover and interior design by Susan Quasha

ISBN: 978-1-58177-159-6
Library of Congress Control Number: 2016908901

Manufactured in the United States of America

To Tian who produces the Dao
To the Dao which produces all things
To all who support me
To all whom I love

CONTENTS

PREFACE

In July 2003, my book *A Detailed Explanation of Laozi: Research on Laozi's Philosophy of Governance* (老子詳解: 老子執政學研究) was published in China. It is now in its fourth printing.

In September 2014, I came to the United States as a research scholar at Harvard University Asia Center to conduct research on Chinese religion and philosophy, and I encountered English versions of the *Dao De Jing* for the first time. I have since browsed more than forty-six different English-language translations, and I have carefully researched eighteen of the more authoritative versions.

What I found is that some of the most important mainland Chinese scholarship with respect to research on the *Dao De Jing* during recent decades has not been incorporated into most of the current English versions, and so I began thinking about composing a completely new translation that would include the latest research. I began this translation project in March of 2015 with the encouragement of Arthur Kleinman and with the help of four American editors: Jacob Lamont Wood, Nancy Hearst, Sam Truitt, and Ron Brent. We completed the work within a year.

The common problems of current English translations of the *Dao De Jing* are enumerated below.

I. The translation of the word 道 (*Dao*)

The 道 (*Dao*) refers to the original source and creator of all things, the source of the natural law of checks and balances, and the power that gives and supports life. However, most of the English translations translate 道 (*Dao*) as the "Way." This is inappropriate for the following reasons.

In Chapter 25 of the *Dao De Jing,* Laozi states: 吾未知其名，字之曰道。吾強為之名曰大 ("I do not know its name and therefore I name it the Dao. I force myself to give it the name Great"). Laozi used the name 道 (*Dao*) and the word 大 (Great) to describe the original source and the natural order of the universe. Chapter 25 expresses the relationship between language and reality in Laozi's philosophy of language. Names or words have no essence on their own; rather, they are guides pointing to reality.

So the words 道 (*Dao*) or 大 (Great) only indicate: they point to the self-existent being, which is infinite and cannot be named or described. The word 道 (*Dao*) has no essence on its own, thus we should not attempt to give it an essentialist meaning: for example, the "Way" or "Way-making."

In everyday Chinese parlance, 道 (*Dao*) has three usages: 道路 (*daolu*), meaning "way"; 説道 (*shuodao*), meaning "speak" or "word"; and 道理 (*daoli*), meaning "principle" or "reason." Which usage may be said to fall closest to the word 道 (*Dao*), which has no essence in itself?

The Chinese pronunciation of 道 is "dao," and this is the best way to express it in English, as this retains its role as just a sign. The *Dao De Jing* begins: "The Dao that can be spoken is not the eternal Dao. The Name that can be named is not the eternal Name." So all efforts to give the word 道 (*Dao*) an essential definition are contrary to the philosophy of language of Laozi.

Some translate *Dao* as "Tao," which is much better than "Way." But this is not an accurate Chinese pinyin pronunciation. In pinyin pronunciation, the "T" is plosive, and the "D" is not plosive. Thus, the most appropriate translation is directly into the Chinese pinyin according to its sound of "Dao."

II. The relationship between 天 (*Tian*) and 道 (*Dao*)

Another common problem with most English translations of the *Dao De Jing* is that they overlook or misinterpret the central relationship in the text between 天 (*Tian*) and 道 (*Dao*).

Tian (天) has two meanings in the *Dao De Jing*: one is the sky; and the other is the divine source and the highest power. In the religious traditions of China's Shang dynasty (ca. 1556–1046 BCE), the highest sovereign divinity was called *Shangdi* (上帝). This was also true in the religious traditions of the Western Zhou dynasty (ca. 1046–771 BCE) and of the Eastern Zhou dynasty (ca. 771–256 BCE), when the highest sovereign divinity was called Shangdi (上帝) or Tian (天). We can translate 天 as "Tian," or we can translate it as "Heaven." In the Chinese religious tradition, "Tian" (Heaven) is the sovereign divine being, which is the creator of all things and is above all natural deities and ancestral spirits. Kingship, for example, was derived from the Mandate of Tian, and only Tian had ultimate power to establish or remove a ruler.

According to the *Records of the Grand Historian* (太史公書), completed during the Han dynasty in about 91 BCE by the historian Sima Qian, Laozi provided lessons to Confucius (551–479 BCE) about the philosophy of rituals. At the time of their meeting, Tian worship was still a royal religious tradition, and it subsequently had a strong spiritual influence in China.

The word *Tian* (天) appears ninety-three times in the *Dao De Jing*. In seventy-four places we may translate it as "sky," but in nineteen places we have to translate it as the heavenly "Tian." The difference between "sky" and "Tian" ("Heaven") is crucial to understanding Laozi, yet most English translations fail to recognize this distinction.

In the *Dao De Jing*, Laozi puts the word "Tian" (天) together with the word "Dao" (道) on eight occasions, such as *Tian Dao* (天道) or *Tian Zhi Dao* (天之道), which can be translated as "The Dao of Tian." In this manner, the Dao comes from Tian, and the Dao is the natural order of the divine Tian. Most people believe that in the *Dao De Jing* the original source and the highest being is the Dao, but this is inaccurate. In the *Dao De Jing*, Tian is the original source and power, and the Dao both comes from Tian and is one with Tian.

III. The challenges facing the various Chinese texts of the *Dao De Jing*

There are many Chinese editions of the *Dao De Jing* text, among which the most popular are the "He Shang Gong" and the "Wang Bi" versions. The He Shang Gong version was commented on by the scholar He Shang Gong, who, according to legend, lived during the reign of Emperor Wen of Han (202–157 BCE). But some scholars, like Yoshio Takeuchi and

Gu Fang, date the He Shang Gong version to about the 3rd century CE. The Wang Bi version was commented on by Wang Bi, who lived later than He Shang Gong, from 226 to 249 CE. Wang Bi was an important philosopher, and his version of the Dao De Jing is the most read in China today. Many of the current English translations of the *Dao De Jing* are based on the Wang Bi version.

The 1973 discovery of the Mawangdui Laozi text A (ca. 202–168 BCE) and the Mawangui Laozi text B (ca. 194–180 BCE) and, subsequently, the Guodian Laozi text (ca. 350–300 BCE) in 1993 have called into question some textual variations in the Wang Bi version. In my book *A Detailed Explanation of Laozi*, I compare the Guodian Laozi and the Mawangdui Laozi versions with the Wang Bi version, summarizing the most important differences. Although there are many variations, most are inconsequential. However, there are twelve core differences that seriously distort the original meaning of the text. For example, Chapter 14 of the Mawangdui texts A and B both state: 執今之道, 以禦今之有 ("Use today's Dao to govern today's reality"). The Wang Bi text changes this to read: 執古之道，以禦今之有 ("Use the ancient *Dao* to govern today's reality"). By changing just one word, from 今 (*Jin*), meaning "today," to 古 (*Gou*), meaning "ancient," the entire meaning is opposite.

Although the Wang Bi version has some obvious issues, it cannot be completely discarded. The Guodian Laozi text is the oldest version of the Laozi text, but it consists of only about 1,744 characters: it is incomplete. Many of the characters in the Mawangdui Laozi text A are damaged, leaving only about 4,089 characters: it is also incomplete. Although the Mawangdui Laozi text B has about 4,833 characters, many of its characters are also damaged and so it cannot be regarded as a complete version. The Mawangdui Laozi texts A and B are not divided by chapters, and the "Book of De" precedes the "Book of Dao." Both the Guodian Laozi text and the Mawangdui Laozi texts A and B have been translated into English, and even though these translations have academic significance, they are not particularly suitable for the reading public. The Wang Bi and the He Shang Gong versions generally have similar chapter divisions, and they both place "The Book of Dao" before "The Book of De"; this format has shaped Chinese readings of the *Dao De Jing* for more than one thousand years. So it is best to retain the divisions in the Wang Bi version and to correct the characters that have been seriously altered in the Guodian Laozi text and the Mawangdui Laozi texts A and B. Therefore, a new version of the Chinese *Dao De Jing* and a new English translation are critically needed.

We refer to this version as a "United" version of the *Dao De Jing*, which is based on contemporary Chinese scholarship, including my own research.

IV. Issues regarding knowledge about political and religious traditions

By returning to the historical background in which Laozi wrote the *Dao De Jing*, we can more accurately understand the meaning of the text. For example, when a new king ascended the throne and appointed ministers, it was customary for him to offer sacrifices on the altar to *Tian* (天) and to implore *Tian* (天) to absolve his sins and bless his kingship. In Chapter 62, Laozi uses such a context to deduce that a king should have compassion for the people. The text reads as follows:

> 故立天子, 置三卿, 雖有拱璧以先四馬, 不如坐進此道。
>
> 古之所以貴此道者何? 不謂 "求以得, 有罪以免" 與? 故為天下貴。

When the son of Tian is enthroned
and the three ministers are appointed
although there is an offering of disks of jade
    before the sacrifice of four horses

it is better for you to sit down and promote this
   teaching from the Dao.
Why was this teaching from the Dao valued by
   the sage rulers in ancient times?
Didn't they say "please answer my supplications
   and forgive me for my sins"?
So this teaching is the most valuable in the world.

As a result of not knowing about the enthroning
ceremony in ancient China—in this case, involving
a king's ritual absolution—all the current English
translations of Chapter 62 of the *Dao De Jing* are
inaccurate. For example, Stephen Mitchell's popular
rendering (*Tao Te Ching*, Harper & Row) of Chapter
62 reads:

> Thus, when a new leader is chosen,
> don't offer to help him
> with your wealth or your expertise.
> Offer instead
> to teach him about the Tao.

In his translation, aside from paring down the text,
Mitchell seems to interpret the jade disks and the four
horses as wealth offered to the new king and the new
high ministers. Laozi, however, uses the new king's
prayer to Tian in the enthronement ("Please answer

my supplications and forgive me for my transgressions") to express his philosophy of good governance. Its essence is to treat others in the same way that you would ask Tian to treat you. In other words, the government should answer the supplications of the people and forgive their sins, which is exactly what a new king asks of Tian. The English translations I have read fail to express this crucial point.

There are similar omissions and errors in many other chapters of the English translations that come from an incomplete understanding of religion and politics in ancient China.

For these reasons, I offer this new "United" version of an English translation of the *Dao De Jing*.

Its abstract style and history of textual variations have made the *Dao De Jing* a wonderfully open system, and this new translation and Chinese version are like streams that flow into the sea of its study. It is my hope this new book will provide readers with an enjoyable experience that truly captures Laozi's philosophy and wisdom.

YANG PENG
Cambridge, Massachusetts

DAO
DE JING

1

The Dao that can be spoken
is not the eternal Dao.
The Name that can be named
is not the eternal Name.
The Nonbeing which cannot be named
is the origin of creation.
The Being which can be named
is the mother of all things.
Being absent of desire
we see the essence of the mystery.
Being full of desire
we see the boundaries of the manifestations.
These two come forth simultaneously
but they are given different names.
The different names point to the same reality.
O   mystery of mysteries
the door to all wonders.

When all the people under the sky know what is
    beautiful
this standard of beauty becomes ugly.
When the entire world knows what is good
this standard of goodness becomes bad.
Being and nonbeing produce each other.
Difficult and easy complement each other.
Long and short contrast each other.
High and low fill each other.
Melody and voice unite each other.
Before and after follow each other.
These are eternal.
So the sage reduces activities of interference
and teaches without speaking.
All things are initiated by themselves.
The sage does not take the initiative.
He acts to eliminate interference and is not
    recorded in history.
He achieves but does not possess success.
He does not claim credit.
Success will never leave him.

3

Do not select and place in power renowned talents
and people will not vie for promotions around you.
Do not value rare and luxurious objects
and people will not become rebels.
Do not reveal desires that can be easily exploited by
     others
and people will not become rebellious and create
     disorder.
This is the self-governance of the sage:
Empty his mind
Fill his belly
Weaken his ambitions
Strengthen his bones.
Always knowing nothing about the sage
people do not desire to make use of him
and those who are cunning dare not conspire.
Act to eliminate interference
and nothing is beyond governance.

4

The Dao is an infinite void
used by all things but never filled to the brim.
O   like a deep valley!
Like the ancestor of all things!
Smoothing all sharp edges
removing all clashes.
Uniting with brilliant light
merging with dark ash.
O   like a boundless sea!
It seems always present.
I do not know whose child the Dao is
but I am certain the Dao existed before all forms
    of gods.

5

The sky and the earth show no partiality toward
    kindness:
they treat all things equally as sacrificial straw dogs.
The sage shows no partiality toward kindness
and treats all people equally as sacrificial straw dogs.
The space between the sky and the earth
is it like a bellows?
Empty but never exhausted
the more it moves
the more it produces.
Listening too much to the ideas of others produces
    failure.
Better to remain neutral and empty.

6

The miraculous fecundity of that Valley never dies.
This is called "the mystical female organ."
The door of the mystical female organ
is called "the root of the sky and the earth."
O   continuous and endless
it seems present.
When used
it is never exhausted.

The sky endures and the earth lasts.
Why can the sky and the earth endure and last?
It is because they are not created by themselves and
    for themselves
they endure and last.
The sage places himself behind
and finds himself in front.
Puts himself outside
to preserve his existence inside.
Is it not because of his unselfishness
that he can realize his real self?

8

The greatest good is like water.
It benefits all things in stillness.
Similar to the Dao
it flows to low places most people abhor.
In living
value the nurturing land.
In your mind
value the emptiness of the valley.
In giving
the generosity of Tian.
In speaking
the keeping of your words.
In politics
good governance.
In handling affairs
ability.
In action
timing.
Do not contend for your own interests
and nobody will hate you.

9

Filling the cup of power to its brim
it is better to stop at the right time.
Hammer a sword until it is over-sharpened
and its edge will not endure.
Fill your home with gold and jade
and you will not be able to safeguard them.
Be arrogant with your power and wealth
and you bring disaster upon yourself.
Withdraw after success:
this is the Dao of Tian.

10

O   can you embrace that One with all your soul
and never depart from it?
Can you concentrate on your breath
to approach the tender state of a newborn?
Can you wash and clean the mysterious mirror in
   your heart
and allow no blemishes on it?
Can you love the people and govern the country
without depending on your own intelligence?
In accordance with the opening and closing of the
   door of Tian
can you bestow rewards and punishments from the
   motherhood?
If your understanding penetrates all sides of the
   earth
can you still keep to the way of not interfering?
Give birth and nourish well.
Produce and do not possess.
Grow and do not control.
This is called the "mystic virtue."

11

Thirty spokes connected to a hub
a hole in the hub to attach the spokes
and we have wheels for the chariots.
Clay is molded into pots.
A cavity in pots
makes them useful.
Doors and windows are cut from walls.
Empty space in a house
makes it habitable.
So what benefit does being provide?
Nonbeing is what we use.

Five colors of cloth blind the eyes.
Five tones of music and dance deafen the ears.
Five flavors of delicious food harm the appetite.
Racing and hunting madden the mind.
Rare and luxurious goods impede right action.
This is the way the sage governs:
He satisfies the real needs of the belly
and never shows to the eyes of others.
So reject that and accept this.

13

A favor is as frightening as a disgrace.
There is great trouble
because there is a body.
What is meant by "a favor is as frightening as a
   disgrace"?
Being favored
lower your mind.
Be afraid
when you receive a favor.
Being out of favor
you have much to fear.
This is the meaning of "a favor is as frightening as
   a disgrace."
What is meant by "there is great trouble because
   there is a body"?
I fear great trouble
because I have my body.
If I had no body
why should I fear?
If you treat the world as you treat your own body
the world can be entrusted to you.
If you love the world as you love your own body
the world can be committed to you.

14

Look
we cannot see it
so we call it Invisible.
Listen
we cannot hear it
so we call it Inaudible.
Seize
we cannot touch it
so we call it Intangible.
These three cannot be measured
so they are united into One.
What is that One?
Above it is not bright.
Below it is not dark.
O   ceaseless and ceaseless
it cannot be named
and returns to nothingness.
We call this the Form of Formlessness
the Image of Nothing
Immense Infinity.
To follow it we cannot see its end.
To meet it we cannot see its beginning.

Use today's Dao to govern today's reality
to know the original beginning.
This is the law of the Dao.

Profound, mysterious and penetrating.
Those who practiced well the Dao in ancient times
Were too deep to be described.
Though they were beyond words
I force myself to describe them.
Cautious like crossing a frozen river in the winter.
Vigilant like fearing hostile neighboring nations on
    four sides.
Respectful like a visiting guest.
Becoming silently loose like ice melting in spring.
Genuine like raw wood.
Mixed like muddy rivers.
Open like the spacious valley.
Who can maintain stillness?
The muddied waters gradually become clear.
Who can remain quiet?
The people will act autonomously
and gradually make a good life for themselves.
Those who follow the way of the Dao
do not fill themselves to the brim.
Because they do not fill themselves to the brim
when trouble arises
they can shield themselves from destruction.

Attain the ultimate emptiness
and concentrate deeply on serenity.
All things emerge together
and I see their repetition.
The Dao of Tian circles endlessly
and everything returns to its roots.
Returning to the roots is called serenity.
Serenity is called "the order of returning."
The order of returning is eternal.
Knowing this eternal order brings bright wisdom.
Not knowing this eternal order brings presumption.
Acting presumptuously is dangerous.
The one who knows this eternal order
can be inclusive.
Inclusive he can be impartial.
Impartial he can be emperor.
Being emperor, he can be as universal as Tian.
As universal as Tian he can walk the path of the
    Dao.
Walking the path of the Dao
he will endure and be free from danger.

17

The best type of governance:
people know that there is a ruler
but never take notice of him.
The next best, people love and praise the ruler.
The next, people fear the ruler.
And the worst, people despise and insult the ruler.
If the ruler does not sufficiently believe in the
     people
the people will not trust him.
O   hesitant
he is very careful when he speaks.
When there are achievements
and people talk about credit
everyone says "I did it on my own."

18

Having abandoned the way of the great Dao
they begin to preach the rule of benevolence and
    loyalty.
When everywhere there is great hypocrisy
they begin to advocate wisdom.
When there is no harmony in the family and among
    relatives
they begin to call for paternal love and filial
    devotion.
When the state falls into confusion and disorder
they begin to emphasize the loyalty of officials.

Reject and renounce

those who flaunt their intellect and like to argue:

people will benefit from it a hundredfold.

Reject and renounce

those who advocate the rule of benevolence and
    loyalty:

people will return to paternal love and filial
    devotion.

Reject and renounce

those who calculate and scheme to increase state
    interests:

there will be no bandits in the country.

If these three things are insufficient

I will give them a foundation:

Express simplicity and embrace the natural.

Reduce your selfishness and diminish your desires.

Reject the knowledge of ritual decorum
and there will be no worries.
"Yes" and "no"
how much difference is there between them?
Good and bad
how much difference is there between them?
Rulers feared by the people
cannot be fearless of the people.
So dissolute their indulgences are without end!
They delight as if enjoying a ritual feast of beef,
    lamb and pork
as if they are in a high garden pavilion in
    springtime.
I am alone and still and reveal no frivolousness
like a newborn that cannot yet smile.
O   so insecure
I feel like a homeless person.
Most people seem to have more than enough
and I alone feel that I am lost.
O   very simple
it seems that I have the heart of a fool.
Most people appear so bright and I alone appear so
    dim.

Most people appear so shrewd and I alone appear
    so dull.

O immense

my heart is like the sea.

O boundless

my mind seems to have no limits.

Most people appear so capable and useful

I alone seem so stubborn and barbaric.

I am different from them.

I only cherish food coming from the motherly Dao.

The great virtue: what does it look like?
It follows only the way of the Dao.
What does the Dao look like?
It is infinite and unlimited.
O   infinite and unlimited
in which there are Forms.
O   unlimited and infinite
in which there are Things.
O   deep and dark
in which is the Essence of Energy.
The Essence of Energy is really true
and there are Constant Laws in it.
From today to the very beginning
its name has not passed away
and it always obeys the Father of creation.
How can I know of the existence of the Father of
    creation?
By these.

22

To twist yourself is to preserve yourself.
To bend yourself is to make yourself upright.
To empty yourself is to fill yourself.
To make yourself obsolete is to renew yourself.
Less is more and more is perplexing.
So the sage who holds to that One
is the shepherd of the world.
He does not regard himself as superior
therefore he is shining.
He does not show himself
therefore he is conspicuous.
He does not take credit for any successes
therefore he is credited with success.
He does not contend for his own interests
therefore no one will contend with him.
"To twist yourself is to preserve yourself."
How can these old sayings be empty words!
Surely, all belongs to him.

23

Aseity speaks few words.
A strong wind never lasts all morning.
A violent rainstorm never endures all day.
What causes these things?
The sky and the earth.
Even the sky and the earth cannot make them last
    for a long time:
how can man?
He who practices the Dao is one with the Dao.
He who follows virtue is one with virtue.
He who transgresses the Dao is one with
    transgression.
He who is one with virtue
is exalted by the Dao.
He who is one with transgression
will be abandoned by the Dao.

24

He who boasts about himself cannot stand firm.

He who regards himself as superior cannot be
    appreciated by others.

He who flaunts himself cannot shine.

He who takes credit for success will not be credited.

He who is self-important cannot endure.

From the standpoint of the Dao

"Extra food is a tumor. It is detested by all."

So he who has great aspirations does not live with
    that.

25

Something like a vast water was formed
before the birth of the sky and the earth.
O   so still and infinite
independent and unchangeable
it can be regarded as the mother of the sky and the
    earth.
I do not know its name
and therefore I name it the Dao.
I force myself to give it the name Great.
"Great" means flowing away.
"Flowing away" means far-reaching.
"Far-reaching" means returning.
The Dao is great.
The sky is great.
The earth is great.
The emperor is also great.
There are four greats in the country
and the emperor is one of them.
Man follows the earth.
The earth follows the sky.
The sky follows the Dao.
And the Dao follows Aseity.

26

Heaviness is the root of lightness.
Stillness is the master of restlessness.
So the man of the Dao marches all day
never leaving his cart with heavy supplies.
Only the minister of national security
reveals such heavy prudence and serious stillness
    even at home.
As the emperor of a great country with ten
    thousand chariots
how can you only pursue bodily desires
and take the destiny of the nation so lightly?
To be light you lose the foundation.
To be restless you lose your mastery.

27

One who is good at leading marches leaves no
    traces of wheels.
One who is good at speaking leaves no flaws to be
    blamed.
One who is good at reckoning uses no counting tools.
One who is good at locking the door needs no
    latches
and the door cannot be opened.
One who is good at knotting uses no ropes
and the knots cannot be untied.
So the sage is always good at saving people.
No one is abandoned and nothing is forsaken.
This is called "following the light."
So the good men are the teachers of the good men
and the bad men are the resources for the good
    man.
Those who do not value their teachers
those who do not love their resources
only have the appearance of wisdom
and in their minds there is great bewilderment.
This is called "the subtle point."

Know the male
but conform to the female
then become the canyon of the world.
Become the canyon of the world
never depart from eternal virtue
and return to the state of a newborn.
Know glory but conform to humility
and become the valley of the world.
Become the valley of the world
filled with eternal virtue
and return to the natural state.
Know the bright but conform to the obscure
and show your respect for the world.
Show your respect for the world
never deviate from eternal virtue
and return to the infinite.
From the free release of the nature of the Dao
all things emanate.
The sage who uses well the free release of the
    nature of all things
becomes the true leader.
Great governance never carves the nature of the
    people.

29

He who acts to obtain the power of the world
I see that he will not get what he wants.
The power of the world is a divine tool
it is bestowed and cannot be gained.
To gain is to fail
to hold is to lose.
So the sage never tries to obtain by himself
thus he will not fail.
He never holds it for his own interests
thus he will not lose.
In front and behind
warm and cold
strong and weak
up and down
all things are interrelated.
So the sage eliminates extremes
arrogance and extravagance.

30

He who assists the lord of men in accordance with
    the Dao
does not coerce the world by force of arms.
The use of military force is usually reciprocated.
Where armies battle
thorns and brambles grow.
Good leaders focus on results
and do not enjoy the advantages of unnecessary
    violence.
Achieve results and do not be proud of yourself.
Achieve results and do not regard yourself as
    superior.
Achieve results and do not claim credit for success.
Achieve results when you have to.
Achieve results without overpowering.
All things begin to grow old
when they reach their apex.
This is called "things that are not the eternal Dao."
He who does not comply with the laws of the Dao
will come to an early end.

Military force is an unpropitious instrument.

It is anathema to all.

The ruler who desires to govern well does not
depend only on it.

A man of Dao values the left side in peacetime at
home

but when he uses armed force he positions himself
at the right side.

Military force is an unpropitious instrument

so it is not a good instrument for the man of Dao

When you are compelled to use armed force

it is better to use surprise attacks as sharp as the
blades of knives.

Do not praise and celebrate the victory of war.

Praising and celebrating the victory of war

means that you love to kill the people.

When you love to kill the people

you cannot realize your aspirations for good
governance in the world.

Auspicious things are put on the left side

inauspicious things are put on the right side.

The position of the lieutenant-general is on the left
the position of the commander-in-chief is on the
    right.
This means that war should be regarded as a
    funeral.
Having killed many people
you should stand and salute them in sorrow.
Having defeated your enemies
you should commemorate the victory with funeral
    rites.

32

The Dao is eternally nameless.
Although the Dao is natural and small
the sky and the earth dare not treat it as
    subservient.
If the marquesses and the emperor keep the Dao
all things will submit spontaneously to the laws of
    the Dao.
When the sky and the earth join
without commands by man
sweet dew falls equally upon everyone.
When you begin to establish institutions
and distribute and name different ranks of power
you should know the limitations of power.
Knowing the limitations of power
you will face no dangers.
The Dao is low in the world
just like the sea is below the rivers and the rivers are
    below the small streams.

33

He who knows others is insightful.

He who knows himself is wise.

He who overcomes others is powerful.

He who overcomes himself is truly strong.

He who is content with himself is rich.

He who is resolute in action has strong willpower.

He who does not lose his nature will endure.

He who lives after death has a long life.

34

O   the great Dao overflows everywhere
to the left and right.
Achieving success and accomplishing all things
the Dao does not claim possession of them.
As all things return to the Dao
and the Dao has no desire to be their master
so we can call the Dao small.
As all things return to the Dao
and the Dao has no desire to be their master
so we can call the Dao great.
The sage can achieve great things.
By never doing great things
he thus achieves great things.

35

Hold to the Great Form
and the world goes toward you.
Going toward you without being harmed
people enjoy security and peace.
Where there is music and fine food
passing travelers will stop to enjoy.
O   the flavor of the words from the Dao is weak
      and tasteless!
Look
you cannot see it.
Listen
you cannot hear it.
When used
it is never exhausted.

36

To blossom is to wither.

To strengthen is to weaken.

To give is to deprive.

To bestow is to remove.

This is called "the dimming light."

The soft and the weak prevail over the hard and the
strong.

Fish cannot leave deep water.

Sharp instruments of state power cannot be
revealed.

37

The Dao never intervenes.
If the marquesses and the emperor cleave to the
    Dao
all things will take a turn for the better.
Taking a turn for the better by themselves
the desires of the people will increase.
I will treat these desires with the non-interference
    of the nameless and natural Dao:
then the people will be satisfied.
When the people are satisfied
they will be at peace
and then all things will be stable by themselves.

A ruler of high virtue does not govern the country
    with the rule of virtue
so he has virtue.
A ruler of low virtue does not abandon the rule of
    virtue
so he has no virtue.
A ruler of high virtue does not intervene:
nothing he does is out of his own self-interest.
The ruler of high personal kindness acts
and his actions are not out of his own self-interest.
The ruler of loyalty acts
and his actions are for his own self-interest.
The ruler of rituals acts and no one responds to
    him
he rolls up his sleeves and drags others.
So when the ruler loses the rule of the Dao
he turns to the rule of virtue.
When the ruler loses the rule of virtue
he turns to the rule of personal kindness.
When the ruler loses the rule of personal kindness
he turns to the rule of loyalty.
When the ruler abandons the rule of loyalty
he turns to the rule of rituals.

So the rule of rituals

is the result of the lack of loyalty and faithfulness

and it marks the beginning of disorder.

Trying to lead the people by your own foresight

is only a flowering illusion about the Dao.

Such rule is most foolish.

Thus a great man dwells in a thick base and not in a
    thin base

in fruits and not in flowers.

So reject that and accept this.

In ancient times they received the power of that
    One.
The sky received it and became clear.
The earth received it and became stable.
The gods received it and became divine.
The valleys received it and became full.
The marquesses and the emperor received it and
    made just laws for the world.
To say this in an extreme way:
Without the power of that One
the sky will have nothing to become clear
and it will break.
The earth will have nothing to become stable
and it will burn.
The gods will have nothing to become divine
and they will come to an end.
The valleys will have nothing to fill them
and they will dry up.
The marquesses and the emperor will have nothing
    to become noble and high
and they will be toppled.
Therefore in order to maintain a noble position
you need a humble foundation.

To maintain high power
you need a low base.
Thus the marquesses and the emperor call
    themselves orphan, widow or barren woman.
Is this not relying on the lowly for the base?
Is this not so?
So the highest praise is to have no praise.
Then do not be as rare and polished as jade
but as common and rugged as rocks.

40

All things return, circle, check, balance and mutually
    transform:
These are the movements of the Dao.
Weak, void, absent obstruction:
These are the uses of the Dao.
All things in the world are born of being
and being is born of nonbeing.

41

When intellectuals of high quality hear of the Dao
they diligently walk in the way of the Dao.
When intellectuals of mediocre quality hear of the
    Dao
they sometimes seem to remember it and
    sometimes seem to forget it.
When intellectuals of low quality hear the Dao
they laugh loudly at it.
If they did not laugh loudly at it
it would not be the Dao.
So there are these sayings in the memorials
    submitted to the throne:
The bright way seems dim.
The way to advance is like retreating.
The broad way seems circuitous.
High virtue is like a valley.
High glory is like humiliation.
Abundant virtue seems to be insufficient.
Creating virtue is like laziness.
True human nature seems to be dirty.
The great square has no corners.
The great power of the nation comes from
    noninterference.

A great melody has almost no sounds.
The form of Tian is formless.
The Dao is great and nameless.
O   it is only the Dao
that can initiate and complete.

42

The Dao gives birth to one.

One gives birth to two.

Two gives birth to three.

Three gives birth to all things.

All things carry Yin on their back and embrace
Yang at their front.

The breath of energy from Yin and Yang compete
with each other

and move toward a balance of harmony.

All people under the sky dislike being an orphan, a
widow or a barren woman

but the emperor and the dukes call themselves by
these names.

So to diminish is to increase

and to increase is to diminish.

The teachings of the sages

I think about them late into the night

and teach them to others.

"A violent strongman will not die a natural death."

I regard this as the beginning of my teaching.

43

The softest things gallop inside the hardest things
    in the world.
The shapeless things enter the most solid things
    that have no crevices.
Therefore I know the benefits of not interfering.
The teaching without speaking
the benefits of not interfering:
the rulers of the world can rarely attain these.

44

A powerful title or your body
which one do you love more?
Your body or your wealth
which one do you cherish more?
Your gain or your loss
which one do you worry about more?
To love too much is to spend too much.
To hoard too much is to lose too much.
Be content and you will not be disgraced.
Knowing when to stop
you will face no dangers and be sustained.

45

Great achievements seem flawed
yet their usefulness is never exhausted.
Great fullness seems empty
yet its usefulness is never ending.
Great straightness seems to bend.
Great skills seem clumsy.
Great earnings seem to pay out.
Warm overcomes cold.
Coolness overcomes heat.
Remain still with non-interference
then you will be the right leader for the world.

46

When the world is governed by the rule of the Dao
the galloping war horses are sent back to fertilize
    the farmland.
When the world is not governed by the rule of the
    Dao
then the war horses will give birth to foals in the
    wilderness.
There is no greater sin than extreme desire.
There is no greater disaster than greediness.
There is no greater risk than insatiability.
So the satisfaction of being content
is the enduring satisfaction.

47

Without taking a step outdoors
I know the entire world.
Without taking a look out the window
I know the Dao of Tian.
The farther you go the less you know.
So the sage knows without walking outside
becomes bright without showing it
and achieves all without interfering.

48

One who pursues learning needs to gain more
   knowledge day by day.
One who follows the Dao needs to reduce acts of
   interference day by day.
Reduce and reduce until you reach the rule of
   noninterference.
Without interference by the ruler all things can be
   accomplished.
To win over the world the ruler should never
   interfere.
If the ruler interferes too much
the country will not be powerful enough to win
   over the world.

49

The sage never has a mind of his own.
He takes the minds of the people as his own.
Those who are kind to me
I am kind to them.
Those who are not kind to me
I am also kind to them.
Then there will be kindness.
Those who trust in me
I trust in them.
Those who do not trust in me
I still trust in them.
Then there will be trust.
O   his mind like muddy water
without making any distinctions
the sage receives all the people of the world.
All the people listen and look at him
and the sage treats himself as their child.

50

There are some people who leave the ways of life
    and enter the ways of death.
Three out of ten are the ways of life.
Three out of ten are the ways of death.
Among those people who practice longevity
one third go to the place of death.
Why is this so?
Because they practice longevity.
I have heard that there are people who know how
    to preserve their lives.
When they walk in the mountains
they do not avoid rhinoceroses and tigers.
When they enter the battlefield
they are not armed with armor and weapons.
The rhinoceroses have nowhere to use their horns
the tigers have nowhere to sink their claws
and wielding weapons have nowhere to use their
    blades.
Why is this so?
Because death has no place in their lives.

51

All things are born of the Dao
reared by the virtue of the Dao
materialized and shaped by the matter of the Dao
functioned and implemented by the effectiveness
    of the Dao.
Therefore all things honor the Dao and venerate its
    virtue.
The honoring of the Dao and the veneration of its
    virtue
are not ennobled and encouraged by any ruler:
they come eternally from the nature of all things.
The Dao produces, rears, grows, fosters, stops and
    poisons.
It is the Dao that nurses and destroys.
The Dao produces but does not possess
accomplishes but does not claim credit.
The Dao grows but does not control.
This is called "the mystical virtue."

52

The world has a beginning
which may be considered to be the mother of all
    things.
After knowing the mother
we may get to know her children.
When we know her children
we should return and cling to the mother.
Then we will never face dangers during our entire
    lives.
Plug your mouth from speaking too much
close your doors to guide the people
and you will never be exhausted.
Opening your mouth to speak a lot
interfering by doing many things
and you will never be saved.
Knowing the smallest thing is called "being
    insightful."
Clinging to softness is called "being strong."
Use the light but return to the source of the light.
Do not lose your life in a disaster.
This is called "following eternity."

53

If I had a small amount of knowledge
I would walk in the way of the great Dao.
I am only afraid of taking the wrong path.
The way of the great Dao is easy
but people prefer the difficult path.
The palace is so well built and kept so clean
but the fields are so desolate
and the warehouses are so empty.
These rulers of the country
dressed in colorful embroidered garments
and carrying sharp swords
are bored with food and drink.
Accumulating more wealth than they can use
they are called "bandit chieftains."
O   they are so Dao-less!

A good founder cannot be uprooted.

A good holder cannot be taken away.

And his children and grandchildren will not stop
    offering sacrifices.

Practice the Dao in oneself and virtue will be true.

Practice the Dao in the family and there will be a
    surplus of virtue.

Practice the Dao in the town and virtue will grow.

Practice the Dao in the state and virtue will be
    abundant.

Practice the Dao in the world and virtue will be
    universal.

Know yourself

then you will know others.

Know your family

then you will know other families.

Know your town

then you will know other towns.

Know your state

then you will know other states.

Know your world

then you will know the world.

How do I know what the world is?
By this.

55

He who is filled with profound virtue is like a
newborn.
Neither wasps nor scorpions nor big or small
snakes will sting him.
Raptors and fierce beasts will not prey upon him.
His bones are weak and his sinews are tender
but his grasp is firm.
Without knowing the union of male and female
his penis becomes angrily erect.
It is because his essence of energy is very strong.
He can cry all day and not be hoarse.
It is because his harmony of balance is great.
The harmony of balance is called "eternal."
Knowing the harmony of balance is called "being
insightful."
Providing benefits to life is called "being auspicious."
Gaining control of one's emotions is called "being
strong."
All things begin aging after reaching their prime.
Trying to reach and maintain one's prime by force
is called "opposing the Dao."
The one who opposes the Dao comes to an early end.

56

He who is wise does not speak.

He who speaks is not wise.

Plug your mouth so as not to speak too much.

Close your doors so as never to interfere.

All sharp edges are filed smooth

all conflicts are resolved

and the brilliant light and the dark ash are merged.

This is called "mystical unity."

So there is no way to receive any impartial love
    from him

and there is no need to be afraid of becoming
    estranged from him.

There is no way to get special interests from him

and there is no need to be afraid of being harmed
    by him.

There is no way to be ennobled by him

and there is no need to be afraid of being disgraced
    by him.

So he is valuable in the world.

Governance of the state should be based on the
    rule of righteousness.

The waging of war should be based on
    unconventional tactics.

To win the world you should follow the way of
    noninterference.

How do I know this to be true?

By this.

The more there are prohibitions the more the
    people will revolt.

The more there are forces of suppression with
    sharp weapons

the more the governance of the state will be
    confused.

The more you use your cleverness

the more evil plots appear.

The more the ritual goods are expanded

the more there will be thieves and bandits.

Therefore these are the words of the sage:

I interfere in nothing

so the people themselves will become rich.

I take no action

so the people themselves will improve.

I prefer stillness
so the people themselves will follow the righteous
way.
I have no desires
so the people will be simple and follow their own
nature.

58

When politics is calm and unexciting
the people will become simple and honest.
When the government is meticulous and strict
the people will become false and cunning.
Misfortune leans on good fortune
and good fortune hides in misfortune.
Who knows where this transformation will end?
So do not force others to follow your standards of
    justice.
Just may become unjust
and good may become evil.
So be upright
but do not cut others.
Be clean
but do not sting others.
Be righteous
but do not intrude upon others.
Be brilliant
but do not dazzle others.
O   the people have been lost for a long time!

59

In governing people and serving Tian
nothing is more important than production.
Only productive power can be called "storing in
    advance."
Storing in advance can be called "valuing the
    accumulation of virtue."
By valuing the accumulation of virtue
there is nothing that you cannot overcome.
When there is nothing that you cannot overcome
no one will know the limits of your power.
When no one knows the limits of your power
you may govern the state.
When the state has power like the love of a mother
governance will last for a long time.
Taproots running deep and fibrous roots remaining
    firm:
this may be called the way for a long life and an
    enduring vision.

60

Governing a great country is like cooking a small fish.
When you govern the world with the rule of the
    Dao
the ghosts will lose their mysterious powers.
It is not that the ghosts will lose their mysterious
    powers
but that their mysterious powers will no longer
    harm humans.
The sage will also not harm humans.
Neither the sage nor the ghosts will do any harm to
    humans
and then together virtue will return to all.

61

A great country is like the low reaches.
It is the mother of the world
where everyone in the world converges.
The female always wins over the male with
    quietness.
Because she is quiet it is good for her to be below.
A large country that humbles itself before a small
    country
wins the support of the small country.
A small country that humbles itself before a large
    country
wins the trust of the large country.
Therefore some humble themselves to win
and some win because they are humble.
Large countries only want to unite and rear more
    people.
Small countries only want to affiliate and serve
    more people.
Both get what they want
and a great country should first humble itself.

62

The Dao is that to which everything flows.
It is the treasure of the good
and is also the refuge of the bad.
When flattering words are sold to you
and respectful manners bring praise upon you
then those people with bad behavior
should they be rejected?
When the son of Tian is enthroned
and the three ministers are appointed
although there is an offering of disks of jade before
the sacrifice of four horses
it is better for you to sit down and promote this
teaching of the Dao.
Why was this teaching of the Dao valued by the
sage rulers in ancient times?
Didn't they say "Please answer my supplications
and forgive me for my transgressions"?
So this teaching is the most valuable in the world.

63

Act to eliminate interference
work to minimize activities
taste what is considered flavorless
make the big small and the many few.
Strive to accomplish a difficult cause through easy
    tasks
and pursue great success from small things.
A difficult cause in the world is accomplished
by implementing easy tasks well.
Great success in the world is achieved
by completing small things well.
The sage never does great things
so he achieves great things.
He who makes promises lightly will lose his
    credibility.
He who changes too much will encounter many
    disasters.
The sage always regards things as too difficult
so he will not face any disasters.

64

That which is in a stable state is easy to control.
That which has not appeared is easy to handle.
That which is at the beginning is easily crushed.
That which is small is easily dispersed.
Act before it comes into being.
Govern before it creates disorder.
A tree as big as the embrace of one's arms
grows from a bud as small as a strand of hair.
A nine-story-high platform is built from mounds of
    dirt.
Standing at a height of hundreds of meters begins
    under your feet.
To intervene is to fail
to control is to lose.
The sage does not want to intervene
so he never fails.
He does not want to control
so he never loses.
People usually fail at the moment when they
    approach their final success
so you should be as careful at the end as you are at
    the beginning
then you will not encounter failure.

Therefore the sage wishes to have no desires to
    interfere
and does not value rare treasures that are difficult to
    obtain.
Teach people without teaching.
Forgive everyone for their mistakes.
Therefore the sage can assist the natural process of
    all things
without daring to interfere in it.

65

He who governs the country with the rule of the
    Dao
does not enlighten the virtue of the people with
    rituals
but lets them simply follow their own natural ways.
People become difficult to govern
when the ruler thinks he is wise.
So he who governs the country with his own
    intelligence
is the one who robs the country.
He who governs the country by thinking he is
    ignorant
is a blessing to the country.
Knowing these two things
you can follow the standard model of the Dao.
Always knowing the standard model of the Dao
is called the "mystic virtue."
The mystic virtue is deep and far-reaching.
Be contrary to mainstream opinions
and then you will attain great success.

66

The rivers and seas are the emperors of the
    hundreds of valley streams
because they are good at remaining below them.
Therefore they become the emperors of the
    hundreds of valley streams.
The sage who is in front of the people
places himself behind the people to follow them.
The sage who is above the people
places himself below the people with humble words.
So when he is in front of the people
the people will not be harmed.
When he is above the people
he will not be a heavy burden on them.
So all the people in the world will like to support
    him
and will not detest him.
Because he does not contend for his own interests
no one will contend with him.

The whole world says that I talk big
and do not follow tradition.
Only when I do not follow tradition
can I become great.
If I had followed tradition
I would have been insignificant for a long time.
I have three treasures:
keep and preserve them.
The first is loving-kindness.
The second is self-restraint.
And the third is daring not to take the initiative
    ahead of the world.
Loving-kindness gives courage.
Self-restraint brings expansion.
And because the ruler dares not to take the initiative
the people's capacity to do things can grow.
Displaying bravery today by abandoning
    loving-kindness
pushing expansion by rejecting self-restraint
and trying to lead the people from the front by
    refusing to follow them from behind:
these are the ways to death.

He who goes to war with loving-kindness will win
the war.

He who defends with loving-kindness will be solid
in his defense.

Tian will establish him and guard him with mercy.

68

A good warrior is not violent.

A good fighter is not angry.

A good conqueror does not engage in battle.

A good leader of men places himself below them.

This is called "the virtue of not-contending."

This is called "the efficient use of human power."

This is called "being matched to the original criteria
of Tian."

69

There is a saying in the art of war:

I dare not be like a host but rather I will be like a
guest.

I dare not advance an inch but rather I will retreat
a yard.

This is called "marching from where there is no road

seizing without arms

controlling without military force."

Then you will be invincible.

No disaster is greater than having no enemy.

It is a danger that will result in losing my valuable
power.

When opposing forces of equal strength fight one
another

the one who regards war as sadness will win.

70

My teachings are easy to know and easy to perform
yet no one knows them and no one performs them.
What I say comes from the Origin.
What I do comes from the Sovereign.
Because people are ignorant, they do not know me.
O   those who know me are few
but those who follow me will be exalted.
Wearing coarse hemp garments
the sage hides jade inside a breast pocket.

71

Knowing that you do not know
is to be sublime.
Not knowing that you do not know
is to be wrong.
The sage is not wrong
because he regards a wrong as a wrong.
Only when you regard a wrong as a wrong
will you not be wrong.

72

When people are no longer afraid of your threats
then a great menace will come upon you.
So do not limit the people's living places
and do not block their livelihood.
Only when you do not oppress the people
Then will people not detest you.
So the sage knows himself and does not show
    himself
loves himself and does not exalt himself.
So leave that and accept this.

73

The one who dares to be bold will be killed.

The one who dares not to be bold will live.

Of these two things one is beneficial and the other
    is harmful.

This is what Tian detests

who knows why?

The Dao of Tian is good at winning without a
    fight.

It responds well without words.

People come to it spontaneously without being
    called.

It is at ease and plans wisely.

The net of Tian extends everywhere.

Although its mesh is wide

nothing can escape it.

74

When people no longer fear death
how can you deter them by killing?
When people's minds are stable and they fear death
if there is someone who engages in rebellion
I will arrest him and kill him:
then who will dare to rebel again?
The death penalty carried out by the permanent
department of justice
is the only lawful killing.
If you substitute by killing on your own
it is called "taking the place of the great artisan to
carve."
He who takes the place of the great artisan to carve
rarely can avoid cutting his own hands.

75

Why are people hungry?
Their ruler above imposes too many taxes
So people are hungry.
Why are people unruly?
Their ruler above interferes too much
and the people are unruly.
Why do the people not care about death?
They strive to have a good life
and they do not care about death.
So not interfering with their lives
better helps them to live.

The newborn is tender and weak
the dead are stiff and hard.
Grass and trees are tender and delicate at birth
but they become withered and dry at death.
So strong and hard are the ways to death
and tender and small are the ways to life.
An army that is too strong and hard will not triumph.
A tree that is too big will be cut down.
So strong and big will be underneath
and tender and small will be above.

The Dao of Tian is like drawing a bow.
Aiming the bow higher
you make the target lower.
Aiming the bow lower
you make the target higher.
You reduce the surplus and add to what is lacking.
So the Dao of Tian reduces the surplus and adds to
    what is lacking.
The way of man is different from that.
It reduces what is lacking and adds to that which
    has a surplus.
Who can offer his surplus to follow and serve Tian?
Only the follower of the Dao?
So the sage serves and does not possess
achieves and does not claim success
has no desire to show his kindness and wisdom.

There is nothing in the whole world
that is softer and weaker than water.
But there is nothing that can surpass water
in attacking the hard and strong
because there is nothing that can change its nature.
The soft prevails over the hard
and the weak prevails over the strong.
All the people in the world know this
but no one can do it.
So the sage says
"The one who bears the humiliation of the country
is to be called the lord of the country.
The one who bears the misfortunes of the country
is to be called the emperor of the world."
Positive words seem to be negative.

79

In reconciling a great hatred
some resentment will surely remain.
How can this be regarded as good?
So the sage holds the left part of a contract as the
    liable person
and he does not demand obligations of others.
He who has virtue
governs the country on the basis of a contract.
He who has no virtue
rules the people by imposing tributes and
    communal work.
The Dao of Tian shows no partiality
and is always with the good person.

May the states be small and each state govern only a
few people.

May the heavy weapons that can only be operated
by tens or hundreds of soldiers never be used.

May people who cherish life avoid being exiled far
away.

May no one ride in war chariots or boats.

May no one display armor or arms.

May people again use knotting cords to keep records.

May people enjoy their delicious food

appreciate their beautiful clothes

be happy with their customs

and be secure in their homes.

Neighboring states see each other:

cocks crow, dogs bark and their sounds can be
heard by each other.

May the people have no wars with one another for
all of their lives.

True words are not beautiful
beautiful words are not true.
The one who knows is not erudite
the one who is erudite does not know.
The good person does not flatter
the one who flatters is not a good person.
The sage does not accumulate and store.
The more he serves others the more he has.
The more he gives to others the more he gains.
The Dao of Tian provides benefits and does not do
    any harm.
The way of the sage acts to accomplish results
but does not contend for his own interests.

道德經
（楊鵬修訂本）

一

道可道，非恒道。名可名，非恒名。無名，萬物
之始。有名，萬物之母。故恒無欲，以觀其妙。
恒有欲，以觀其徼。兩者同出，異名同謂。玄之
又玄，眾妙之門。

二

天下皆知美之為美，斯惡已。皆知善之為善，
斯不善已。有無相生，難易相成，長短相形，
高下相盈，音聲相和，前後相隨，恒也。是以聖
人居無為之事，行不言之教。萬物作而弗始，
為而弗志，功成而弗居。夫唯弗居，是以不去。

三

不上賢，使民不爭。不貴難得之貨，使民不為
盜。不見可欲，使民不亂。是以聖人之治：
虛其心，實其腹，弱其志，強其骨。恒使民無知
無欲，使夫智者不敢為也。為無為，則無不治。

四

道沖，而用之或不盈。淵呵！似萬物之宗。銼其
銳，解其紛。和其光，同其塵。湛呵！似或存。
吾不知其誰之子。象帝之先。

五

天地不仁，以萬物為芻狗。聖人不仁，以百姓為
芻狗。天地之間，其猶橐籥乎？虛而不屈，動而
愈出。多聞數窮，不如守於中。

六

浴神不死，是謂玄牝。玄牝之門，是謂天地之根。
綿綿呵！其若存。用之不勤。

七

天長地久。天地所以能長且久者，以其不自生，
故能長生。是以聖人後其身而身先，外其身而身
存。非以其無私輿？故能成其私。

八

上善若水。水善利萬物而有靜。居眾人之所惡，
故幾於道。居善地，心善淵，予善天，言善信，
政善治，事善能，動善時。夫唯不爭，故無尤。

九

持而盈之，不如其已。揣而銳之，不可長保。金
玉盈室，莫之能守。貴富而驕，自遺其咎。功遂
身退，天之道也。

十

載營魄抱一，能無離乎？專氣致柔，能嬰兒乎？
滌除玄鑒，能無疵乎？愛民治國，能無以知乎？
天門開闔，能為雌乎？明白四達，能無為乎？
生之畜之。生而不有，長而不宰，是謂玄德。

十一

三十輻，共一轂。當其無，有車之用。埏埴而為
器。當其無，有埴器之用。鑿戶牖。當其無，
有室之用。故有之以為利，無之以為用。

十二

五色使人目盲。五音使人耳聾。五味使人口爽。
馳騁田獵使人心發狂。難得之貨使人行妨。是以
聖人之治也，為腹不為目。故去彼取此。

十三

寵辱若驚。貴大患若身。何謂寵辱若驚？寵之為
下。得之若驚，失之若驚，是謂寵辱若驚。何謂
貴大患若身？吾所以有大患者，為吾有身。及吾
無身，吾有何患？故貴為身於為天下，若可托天
下。愛以身為天下，若可寄天下。

十四

視之不見，名之曰微。聽之不聞，名之曰希。搏
之不得，名之曰夷。此三者不可至計，故混而為
一。其上不曒，在下不昧。繩繩呵不可名，複歸
於無物。是謂無狀之狀，無物之象，是謂沕望。
隨而不見其後，迎而不見其首。執今之道，以禦
今之有，以知古始，是謂道紀。

十五

古之善為道者，微妙玄達，深不可志。夫唯不可志，故強為之容：豫呵其若冬涉水。猶呵其若畏四鄰。嚴呵其若客。渙呵其若淩釋。敦呵其若樸。混呵其若濁。曠呵其若浴。孰能濁而靜之，將徐清。孰能安以動之，將徐生。保此道者，不欲盈。夫唯不欲盈，是以能敝而不成。

十六

致虛極，守靜篤。萬物並作，吾以觀複。天道員員，各複歸其根。歸根曰靜。靜曰覆命。覆命常也，知常明也。不知常，妄作凶。知常容，容乃公，公乃王，王乃天，天乃道，道乃久，沒身不殆。

十七

太上，下知有之。其次，親譽之。其次，畏之。
其下，侮之。信不足，有不信焉。猶呵其貴言！
成事述功，百姓皆謂：我自然。

十八

大道廢，有仁義。智慧出，有大偽。六親不和，
有孝慈。國家昏亂，有忠臣。

十九

絕智棄辯，民利百倍。絕仁棄義，民複孝慈。
絕巧棄利，盜賊無有。此三者以為使不足，故令
之有所屬：見素抱樸，少私寡欲。

二十

絕學無憂。唯之與訶，相去幾何？美之與惡，相去何若？人之所畏，亦不可不畏人。荒呵其未央哉！眾人熙熙，若享太牢，而春登臺。我泊焉未佻，若嬰兒之未咳。累累呵，似無所歸。眾人皆有餘，而我獨若遺。我愚人之心也，沌沌呵！俗人昭昭，我獨昏昏。俗人察察，我獨悶悶。沕呵，其若海。望呵，其若無所止。眾人皆有以，我獨頑且鄙。我獨異於人，而貴食母。

二十一

孔德之容，唯道是從。道之為物，唯望唯沕。沕呵望呵，其中有象。望呵沕呵，其中有物。窈呵冥呵，其中有精。其精甚真，其中有信。自今及古，其名不去，以順眾父。吾何以知眾父之然也？以此。

二十二

曲則全，枉則正，窪則盈，敝則新，少則多，多則惑。是以聖人執一，以為天下牧。不自視，故明。不自見，故彰。不自伐，故有功。不自矜，故能長。夫唯不爭，故莫能與之爭。古之所謂"曲則全"者，豈虛語哉！誠全歸之。

二十三

希言自然。飄風不終朝，暴雨不終日。孰為此者？天地。天地而不能久，而況於人乎！故從事於道者，同於道。德者，同於德。失者，同於失。同於德者，道亦德之。同於失者，道亦失之。

二十四

炊者不立。自視者不彰。自見者不明。自伐者無功。自矜者不長。其在道也，曰：餘食贅形，物或惡之。故有欲者弗居。

二十五

有物混成，先天地生。寂呵寥呵，獨立而不改，可以為天地母。吾未知其名，字之曰道。吾強為之名曰大。大曰逝，逝曰遠，遠曰反。道大，天大，地大，王亦大。國中有四大，而王居一焉。人法地，地法天，天法道，道法自然。

二十六

重為輕根，靜為躁君。是以君子終日行，不離其輜重。唯有環官，燕處則昭若。奈何萬乘之王，而以身輕於天下？輕則失本，躁則失君。

二十七

善行者無轍跡。善言者無瑕謫。善數者不用籌策。善閉者無關楗而不可開。善結者無繩約而不可解。是以聖人恒善救人而無棄人，物無棄材，是謂襲明。故善人者，善人之師。不善人者，善人之資。不貴其師，不愛其資，雖智大迷。是謂要妙。

二十八

知其雄，守其雌，為天下溪。為天下溪，恒德不離，複歸於嬰兒。知其榮，守其辱，為天下浴。為天下浴，恒德乃足，複歸於樸。知其白，守其黑，為天下式。為天下式，恒德不忒，複歸於無極。樸散則為器，聖人用之，則為官長。夫大制不割。

二十九

將欲取天下而為之，吾見其不得已。夫天下神器，非可為者也。為之者敗之，執之者失之。是以聖人無為，故無敗。無執，故無失。物或行或隨，或熱或吹，或強或羸，或陪或墮。是以聖人去甚去大去奢。

三十

以道佐人主，不以兵強於天下。其事好還。師之
所處，荊棘生之。善者果而已，不以取強。果而
勿驕，果而勿矜，果而勿伐，果而不得已，果而
勿強。物壯則老，謂之不道。不道早已。

三十一

夫兵者，不祥之器，物或惡之，故有欲者弗居。
君子居則貴左，用兵則貴右。故兵者非君子之器
也。兵者不祥之器也，不得已而用之，銛襲為上。
勿美也。若美之，是樂殺人也。夫樂殺人，則不
可得志於天下矣。吉事上左，喪事上右，是以偏
將軍居左，上將軍居右，言以喪禮處之。殺人
眾，以悲哀立之。戰勝，以喪禮處之。

三十二

道恒無名。樸雖小，而天地弗敢臣。侯王能守之，萬物將自賓。天地相合，以降甘露，民莫之令而自均。始制有名，名亦既有，夫亦將知止，知止所以不殆。卑道之在天下，猶小浴之與江海也。

三十三

知人者智，自知者明。勝人者有力，自勝者強。知足者富。強行者有志。不失其所者久。死而不亡者壽。

三十四

大道汜呵，其可左右也。成功逐事而弗名有，萬物歸焉而弗為主，則恒無欲也，可名於小。萬物歸焉而弗為主，可名於大。是以聖人之能成大也，以其不為大也，故能成其大。

三十五

執大象，天下往。往而不害，安平太。樂與餌，過客止。道之出言，淡呵其無味也。視之不足見，聽之不足聞，用之不可既也。

三十六

將欲歙之，必固張之。將欲弱之，必固強之。將欲去之，必固與之。將欲奪之，必固予之。是謂微明。柔弱勝剛強。魚不可脫於淵，國之利器不可以示人。

三十七

道恒無為。侯王能守之，萬物將自化。化而欲作，吾將貞之以無名之樸，夫亦將知足。知足以靜，萬物將自定。

三十八

上德不德，是以有德。下德不失德，是以無德。上德無為而無以為。上仁為之而無以為。上義為之而有以為。上禮為之而莫之應，則攘臂而扔之。故失道而後德，失德而後仁，失仁而後義，失義而後禮。夫禮者，忠信之薄，而亂之首也。前識者，道之華，而愚之首也。是以大丈夫居其厚而不居其薄，居其實而不居其華。故去彼而取此。

三十九

昔之得一者：天得一以清，地得一以寧，神得一以靈，浴得一以盈，侯王得一而以為天下正。其至也，謂天無以清，將恐裂。地無以寧，將恐發。神無以靈，將恐歇。浴無以盈，將恐竭。侯王無以貴以高，將恐蹶。故必貴，而以賤為本。必高矣，而以下為基。夫是以侯王自謂孤寡不穀。此非以賤為本與？非也？故至譽無譽。是故，不欲祿祿如玉，硌硌如石。

四十

反也者，道之動。弱也者，道之用。天下之物生
於有，有生於無。

四十一

上士聞道，勤能行之。中士聞之，若存若忘。
下士聞道，大笑之。弗大笑，不足以為道。是以
建言有之曰：明道如昧。進道如退。夷道如纇。
上德如浴。大白如辱。廣德如不足。建德如偷。
質真如渝。大方無隅。大器免成。大音希聲。天
象無形。道褒無名。夫唯道，善始且善成。

四十二

道生一，一生二，二生三，三生萬物。萬物負陰
而抱陽，沖氣以為和。天下之所惡，唯孤、寡、
不穀，而王公以自名也。物或損之而益，或益之
而損。人之所教，夕議而教人。強梁者不得其
死，吾將以為教父。

四十三

天下之至柔，馳騁於天下之至堅。無有入於無間。
吾是以知無為之有益也。不言之教，無為之益，
天下希能及之矣。

四十四

名與身孰親？身與貨孰多？得與亡孰病？甚愛必
大費，多藏必厚亡。故知足不辱，知止不殆，可
以長久。

四十五

大成若缺，其用不弊。大盈若沖，其用不窮。大
直若屈，大巧若拙，大贏若肭。躁勝寒，靜勝
熱。清靜可以為天下正。

四十六

天下有道，卻走馬以糞。天下無道，戎馬生於郊。
罪莫大於甚欲，咎莫險於欲得，禍莫大於不知
足。故知足之為足，恒足矣。

四十七

不出於戶，以知天下。不窺於牖，以知天道。
其出彌遠者，其知彌少。是以聖人不行而知，
不見而明，不為而成。

四十八

為學者日益，為道者日損。損之又損，以至於無
為。無為而無不為。取天下也，恒無事。及其有
事也，不足以取天下。

四十九

聖人無恒心，以百姓心為心。善者，吾善之。
不善者，吾亦善之，德善也。信者，吾信之。
不信者，吾亦信之，德信也。聖人在天下，歙歙
焉，為天下渾心。百姓皆屬耳目焉，聖人皆孩之。

五十

出生入死。生之徒，十有三。死之徒，十有三。
而民生生，動皆之死地，亦十有三。夫何故？以
其生生。蓋聞善執生者，陵行不避兕虎，入軍不
被甲兵。兕無所投其角，虎無所措其爪，兵無所
容其刃。夫何故？以其無死地。

五十一

道生之而德畜之，物形之而器成之。是以萬物尊
道而貴德。道之尊，德之貴，夫莫之爵而恒自
然。道生之畜之，長之育之，亭之毒之，養之覆
之。生而不有，為而不恃，長而不宰。是謂玄
德。

五十二

天下有始，以為天下母。既得其母，以知其子。
既知其子，複守其母，沒身不殆。塞其兌，閉其
門，終身不勤。啟其兌，濟其事，終身不救。
見小曰明，守柔曰強。用其光，複歸其明，無遺
身殃，是謂襲常。

五十三

使我介有知，行于大道，唯施是畏。大道甚夷，
而人好徑。朝甚除，田甚蕪，倉甚虛。服文采，
帶利劍，厭飲食，財貨有餘。是謂盜竽，非道也
哉！

五十四

善建者不拔，善抱者不脫，子孫以祭祀不絕。
修之身，其德乃真。修之家，其德乃餘。修之鄉，
其德乃長。修之國，其德乃豐。修之天下，其德
乃博。以身觀身，以家觀家，以鄉觀鄉，以國觀
國，以天下觀天下。吾所以知天下之然哉？以
此。

五十五

含德之厚者，比於赤子。蜂蠆虺蛇不螫，攫鳥猛
獸不搏。骨弱筋柔而握固，未知牝牡之合而朘
怒，精之至也。終日號而不憂，和之至也。和曰
常。知和曰明。益生曰祥。心使氣曰強。物壯則
老，謂之不道。不道早已。

五十六

知者不言，言者不知。塞其兌，閉其門。銼其
銳，解其紛。和其光，同其塵。是謂玄同。故不
可得而親，不可得而疏，不可得而利，不可得而
害，不可得而貴，不可得而賤，故為天下貴。

五十七

以正治國，以奇用兵，以無事取天下。吾所以知
其然也？以此。天下多忌諱而民彌畔。民多利器
而國家滋昏。人多知而奇物滋起。法物滋彰而盜
賊多有。是以聖人之言曰：我無事而民自富，我
無為而民自化，我好靜而民自正，我無欲而民自
樸。

五十八

其政悶悶，其民淳淳。其政察察，其民缺缺。
禍兮福所倚，福兮禍所伏。孰知其極？其無正也。
正複為奇，善複為妖。是以方而不割，廉而不
刺，直而不肆，光而不耀。人之迷，其日固久。

五十九

治人事天，莫若嗇。夫唯嗇，是謂早備。早備謂
之重積德。重積德則無不克。無不克則莫知其
極。莫知其極，可以有國。有國之母，可以長
久。是謂深根固柢，長生久視之道。

六十

治大國，若烹小鮮。以道立天下，其鬼不神。
非其鬼不神，其神不傷人。聖人亦不傷人。夫兩
不相傷，故德交歸焉。

六十一

大國者下流。天下之牝，天下之交也。牝恒以靜
勝牡。為其靜也，故宜為下。大國以下小邦，
則取小國。小國以下大國，則取於大國。故或下
以取，或下而取。大國不過欲兼畜人，小國不過
欲入事人。夫皆得其欲，則大者宜為下。

六十二

道者萬物之注也。善人之寶，不善人之所保。
美言可以市，尊行可以賀人，人之不善，何棄之
有？故立天子，置三卿，雖有拱璧以先四馬，
不如坐進此道。古之所以貴此道者何？不謂
"求以得，有罪以免"與? 故為天下貴。

六十三

為無為，事無事，味無味，大小多少。圖難於其
易，為大於其細。天下難事必作于易，天下大事
必作於細。是以聖人終不為大，故能成其大。夫
輕諾必寡信，多易必多難。是以聖人猶難之，故
終無難矣。

六十四

其安易持，其未兆易謀。其脆易泮，其微易散。
為之於未有，治之於未亂。合抱之木，生於毫
末。九層之台，起於累土。百仞之高，始於足
下。為者敗之，執者失之。是以聖人無為故無
敗，無執故無失。民之從事，常于幾成而敗之。
慎終如始，則無敗事。是以聖人欲不欲，不貴難
得之貨。教不教，複眾人之所過。是故聖人能輔
萬物之自然而不敢為。

六十五

為道者非以明民，將以愚之。民之難治，以其智也。故以智治國，國之賊也。不以智治國，國之福也。知此兩者亦稽式。恒知稽式，此謂玄德。玄德深矣遠矣，與物反矣，乃至大順。

六十六

江海所以能為百浴王者，以其善下之，是以能為百浴王。聖人之在民前也，必以身後之。其在民上也，必以言下之。故居前而民弗害，居上而民弗重，是以天下樂推而不厭。以其不爭也，故天下莫能與之爭。

六十七

天下皆謂我大。大而不肖。夫唯不肖,故能大。若肖,細久矣!我恒有三寶,持而保之。一曰慈,二曰儉,三曰不敢為天下先。慈故能勇。儉故能廣。不敢為天下先,故能為成事長。今舍慈且勇,舍儉且廣,舍後且先,則必死矣!夫慈以戰則勝,以守則固。天將建之,以慈衛之。

六十八

善為士者不武。善戰者不怒。善勝敵者不與。善用人者為之下。是謂不爭之德,是謂用人之力,是謂天古之極。

六十九

用兵有言:吾不敢為主而為客。不敢進寸而退尺。是謂行無行,攘無臂,扔無敵,執無兵,乃無敵矣。禍莫大於無敵,無敵幾喪吾寶。故抗兵相若,哀者勝矣。

七十

吾言甚易知，甚易行。天下莫之能知，莫之能行。言有宗，事有君。夫唯無知，是以不我知。知我者希，則我者貴。是以聖人被褐而懷玉。

七十一

知不知，尚矣。不知知，病也。聖人不病，以其病病。夫唯病病，是以不病。

七十二

民不畏威，則大威至。無狎其所居，無厭其所生。夫唯不厭，是以不厭。是以聖人自知而不自見，自愛而不自貴。故去彼取此。

七十三

勇於敢則殺，勇於不敢則活。此兩者，或利或
害。天之所惡，孰知其故？天之道，不戰而善
勝，不言而善應，不召而自來，繟然而善謀。天
網恢恢，疏而不失。

七十四

民不畏死，奈何以殺懼之？若民恆且畏死，而為
奇者，吾得而殺之，夫孰敢矣？恆有司殺者殺。
夫代司殺者殺，是代大匠斲。夫代大匠斲者，稀
有不傷其手矣。

七十五

民之饑，以其上食稅之多，是以饑。百姓之不治，
以其上有以為，是以不治。民之輕死，以其求生
之厚，是以輕死。夫唯無以生為者，是賢貴生。

七十六

人之生也柔弱，其死也堅強。草木之生也柔脆，其死也枯槁。故堅強者死之徒，柔弱微細生之徒。是以兵強則不勝，木強則折。強大處下，柔弱處上。

七十七

天之道，猶張弓也。高者抑之，下者舉之。有餘者損之，不足者補之。故天之道，損有餘而益不足。人之道則不然，損不足而奉有餘。孰能有餘而有以取奉於天者？唯有道者乎？是以聖人為而不有，成功而不居，其不欲見賢也。

七十八

天下莫柔弱于水，而攻堅強者莫之能勝，以其無以易之。柔之勝剛，弱之勝強，天下莫不知，而莫能行。故聖人之言曰：受國之垢，是謂社稷之主。受國之不祥，是謂天下之王。正言若反。

七十九

和大怨，必有餘怨，焉可以為善？是以聖人執左
契，而不責於人。有德司契，無德司徹。天道無
親，恒與善人。

八十

小國寡民。使十百人之器勿用，使民重死而遠
徙。有車舟無所乘之，有甲兵無所陳之。使民複
結繩而用之。甘其食，美其服，樂其俗，安其
居。鄰國相望，雞狗之聲相聞。民至老死，不相
往來。

八十一

信言不美，美言不信。知者不博，博者不知。
善者不多，多者不善。聖人無積，既以為人己愈
有，既以予人己愈多。故天之道，利而不害。
人之道，為而不爭。

ABOUT THE AUTHOR

LAOZI, a great sage of ancient China, was the author of the *Dao De Jing* and the founder of Daoism. According to *The Records of the Grand Historian* (太史公書), finished around 91 BCE, Laozi was a contemporary of Confucius (551–479 BCE) to whom the elder Laozi gave lessons about the philosophy of rituals. Laozi worked as the official historian and the keeper of the archives at the imperial court of the Zhou dynasty. At that time, the official historian drafted government documents and played the role of astrologer and teacher of the religious rituals. Laozi uses the word "Dao" to describe the original and natural law he discovered. Because the Dao is the original and fundamental power and the natural law, which is always universal, creative, productive, and harmonious, the core of good governance is to reduce and minimize interference, allowing the power of the Dao to release its great productive and harmonious potentiality freely from everyone and everything. Prosperity and harmony only come from government non-interference and self-governance by the individual and the people. The wisdom of Laozi is a valuable and spiritual treasure of mankind.

ABOUT THE TRANSLATOR

Born in China in 1963, YANG
PENG is a scholar of Daoism
and Chinese religions and
regarded as one of the repre-
sentatives of Neo-Daoism in
China today. He is the author
of five books, including *A
Detailed Explanation of Laozi: Research on Laozi's Philos-
ophy of Governance* and *The Origin of Shangdi Worship
in China,* which have had a wide audience and influ-
ence. Yang Peng is currently a research scholar at the
Harvard University Asia Center.

ABOUT WAPNER & BRENT BOOKS

Wapner & Brent Books is the publishing arm of Asia Arts and Culture, LLC, a partnership between book developer Kenneth Wapner and entrepreneur-consultant Ron Brent.

Our primary mission is to develop and publish books introducing some of Asia's most dynamic spiritual, cultural and artistic traditions. Of particular interest are new voices that have yet to be heard in the United States and abroad.